FARM CHARM

In the FIELD

by Pearl Markovics

Consultant:
Beth Gambro
Reading Specialist
Yorkville, Illinois

Contents

BEARPORT PUBLISHING
New York, New York

In the Field

Look around.

What do you see?

I see cows in the field.

What do you see?

I see birds in the field.

What do you see?

I see flowers in the field.

What do you see?

I see horses in the field.

What do you see?

I see butterflies in the field.

Look closely!